WORK AND PLAY

Written by Sydnie Meltzer Kleinhenz • Illustrated by Mick Reasor

Children's Press®
A Division of Scholastic Inc.
New York • Toronto • London • Auckland • Sydney
Mexico City • New Delhi • Hong Kong
Danbury, Connecticut

To the Houston chapter of the Society of Children's Book Writers and Illustrators, for their nurturing and support.
— S.M.K.

To Lark
— M.R.

Consultant

Eileen Robinson
Reading Specialist

Library of Congress Cataloging-in-Publication Data
Meltzer Kleinhenz, Sydnie
  Work and play / written by Sydnie Meltzer Kleinhenz ; illustrated by Mick Reasor.
      p. cm. — (A Rookie reader)
  Summary: A girl looks at different jobs as she thinks about what
she might do someday.
  ISBN 0-516-24433-7 (lib. bdg.)   0-516-25282-8 (pbk.)
  [1. Occupations—Fiction. 2. Stories in rhyme.] I. Reasor, Mick, ill. II. Title. III. Series.
  PZ8.3.K675Wo 2004
  [E]—dc22

                                        2004009327

CHILDREN'S PRESS, and A ROOKIE READER®, and associated logos are trademarks
and or registered trademarks of Scholastic Library Publishing. SCHOLASTIC and
associated logos are trademarks and or registered trademarks of Scholastic Inc.
1 2 3 4 5 6 7 8 9 10 R 14 13 12 11 10 09 08 07 06 05

People work in inside places.

3

People work in outside spaces.

5

People work in morning light.

People work in dark at night.

People work above the street.

People work below my feet.

13

People work in cold or heat.

People work to buy or sell.

I have work I do as well.

Are things I do at school
and play...

like work that I may do someday?

Word List (38 words)

above	feet	my	spaces
and	have	night	street
are	heat	or	that
as	I	outside	the
at	in	people	things
below	inside	places	to
buy	light	play	well
cold	like	school	work
dark	may	sell	
do	morning	someday	

About the Author

Sydnie Meltzer Kleinhenz teaches kindergarten in Houston, Texas. She lives with a dog, a one-legged parakeet, and numerous reptiles, amphibians, and fish. She also has five loveable sons. Her published credits include many poems, magazine articles, and over 50 books for store sales and school curriculums.

About the Illustrator

Mick Reasor is an artist, teacher, and husband, and father of four brilliant girls. He lives, works, and plays in Grand Rapids, Minnesota.